THE FA

New War Poetry
For A Changing World

Stephan J Myers

An assembly of verses about war. Based on the thoughts and true stories of soldiers, war widows, parents, lovers and children for whom war irrevocably changed their lives.

PUBLISHER | KRONOS PUBLISHING LONDON

1st Edition published by Kronos Publishing Ltd. 2023

Published in Great Britain in 2018 by
Kronos Publishing Limited
Reg. No. 10543850

A CIP catalogue record for this book is available
from the British Library

Paperback ISBN 978-1-9999420-4-5

For all those who have fallen.
Words can never truly convey the debt of gratitude
we forever owe you.

Contents

Bonus Poems From Thief Of Hearts

The briefest of introductions.........

I can't speak for other poets but with every poem I write I am drawn to a thought or sentiment of my own making. However, in penning the war poems for The Fallen I found myself in uncharted waters; drawn to an idea but giving voice to the thoughts of others.

With the advent of social media, images of conflict are more prevalent now than ever before. Hauntingly powerful, damming, forever eroding the base of our humanity, yet still we go to war.

Several prolific poets and authors have tackled the subject of war in their works: Siegfried Sassoon, Wilfred Owen, Rupert Brookes and Rudyard Kipling. Some approaching it in a direct, brutally hard-hitting manner, whilst others have adopted the subtleties of satire.

It's my belief that the only people fit to comment on war are those it directly affects: Those who bear arms, those who have lost loved ones, and those who live with the aftermath of whole-scale carnage.

The Fallen was written for those who have served and made the ultimate sacrifice so that we might embrace our freedom and the men and women who have served and survived. The war poems written are reflections of conversations Pixie Woodstock and I have had with those who have lost husbands, wives, lovers, brothers, sisters, sons and daughters. Heart-rending, revealing and often surprising, they relate to conflicts past and present.

Perceptions change depending on our experiences and through the openness of those we had the privilege of speaking to, we set out to write poems that portray the many facets and legacy of war.

We have explored PTSD, honour, duty, heroism, the darkest of thoughts, regrets, loss and betrayal. And throughout we were reminded that the impact of war on those closest to our serving men and women should never be forgotten.

The poems are neither pro nor anti-war but simply the sum of thoughts from those fittest to comment. Some are inspired by letters to loved ones we were privileged to read, many from the first and second World Wars. Whatever your view on war, all we ask is you read the poems with an open mind and appreciate the differing perspectives.

As with Thief Of Hearts, the majority of poems within aren't fleeting, but are interceded with quotes and thoughts which aim to capture the sentiment of the collection.

I hope that with these words we touch your heart and mind. That somewhere along this journey we call life our thoughts will briefly bring us together and the sacrifices of so many will never be forgotten.

And finally, my unerring thanks to the elusive Pixie Woodstock whose words never fail to bring the extraordinary to life.

*"To walk amongst, but now apart.
A fractured life in fits and starts."*

Trauma changes the way we view life and often shatters our most basic assumptions about ourselves and the world about us.

Soldiers suffering from PTSD don't ask their mind to rewind and replay their experiences in flashback form and when going through extended periods of trauma it becomes increasingly difficult to relate to the normalcy of everyday life as the horrors of war return to haunt them.

Pixie Woodstock

Darkest Thoughts

I   This cage of mind corralled by night,
that courts dark thoughts and craves the light.

Where shadows wane but not my guilt,
for by my hand much blood was spilt.

II   The rattle that proclaims a death.
The haunting sound of man's last breath.

And I like them each day unknown,
no goodness there in actions shown.

III   Such faith had I now long defiled.
No more a man so wise and mild.

Sullied now by wars warped rite,
my broken soul denied the light.

IV   Not now red sands beneath my feet.
Once more returned to Civvy Street.

To walk amongst, but now apart.
A fractured life in fits and starts.

v   To dread the ravishes of night.
My mind adrift and phantoms fight.

Such horrors spawned when blood is spilt.
My soul denied respite from guilt.

VI   For shadows plague my waking hours,
memories from which I cower.

A constant battle in my head,
for I draw breath whilst friends lie dead.

VII   Unforgiving unrelenting,
horrors that are unrepenting.

My sanity to cleave to shreds,
as war continues in my head.

VIII   The wails the screams and flailing limbs,
with terrors such my mind now swims.

Such ends that human hands have wrought,
now dominate my waking thoughts.

IX   Each one demands a vigil keep,
and know no more a peaceful sleep.

With night immersed in hopeless pain,
recalling faces long now slain.

X   My mind a warring night and day.
For sufferings respite I pray.

To me this life is like a tomb,
where joy and hope no longer bloom.

"My comrades brave,
with babes and wives.
Torn to shreds
before my eyes."

Older men declare war but it is the young that bear arms and come to know the true horror of events that shatter our most valued assumptions about ourselves and the world in which we live.

Stephan J Myers

PTSD

I His baby breath
hung milky white.
    Soft downy hair
    within my sight.

But as I bent to
kiss his head.
    Behind my eyes
    the horror spread.

III The acrid smoke
of bullets past.
    The stench of blood,
    gut wrenching blast.

The begging eyes,
and smell of fear.
    Hands clutching hope
    on coming near.

V His soapy skin,
flushed pink and new.
    Eyes clear and bright
    with mother's hue.

VI   Softest skin and
gurgling smile.
Now overspread
by all things vile.

With shaking hands
and eyes shut tight.
Memories of each
haunting sight.

VIII My comrades brave
with babes and wives.
Torn to shreds
before my eyes.

As tears spill out to
soak his head.
I gently lay him
down to bed.

X   Watch softly as he
sucks his thumb.
And pray for all
the orphaned young.

"I dream of you amidst the fray.
A heavy price for war we pay."

For military partners awaiting the return of their loved ones hope is the ember that awaits a spark; the tiniest spark to ignite the flame that will carry them through the darkness of separation.

Stephan J Myers

The Memory Of You

I   Ripped apart from you I cry.
With soulless eyes search empty sky.

      The blank moon casts its mocking gaze,
concealing stars with ghoulish glaze.

III   My bed grows huge and sucks me down,
to safety steal and pleasure drown.

      Within the cool of linen sheets,
no breath to share or lips to meet.

V   I dream of you amidst the fray;
a heavy price for war we pay.

      Our time so swift not meant to last,
an errant spell our fates did cast.

VII   In numbing solitude I stare,
as if to turn and find you there.

      With trembling limbs turned waxy blue,
I lay like death and think of you.

Claxons Wail

I   Sodium lit and fresh scrubbed halls,
claxons wail as voices call.
        Comrades waiting silent stand,
        embracing lest they fall.

II   Twist of fate that each must share,
sanctity of fates grand plan.
        Revealed in time to each and all;
        woman, mother, father, man.

III   Voices die and heavy steps,
silence fuels the news they dread.
        Behind closed doors a battle lost,
        on scrubs a spot of red.

IV   Teetering, listing, moments past,
a chapter finds its end.
        Fated brother, husband, son,
        confidant and truest friend.

V   Sodium lit and fresh scrubbed halls,
claxons wail as voices call.
        Soldiers weary silent stand,
        embracing lest they fall.

"In endless regimented rows.
Beneath the silver stars."

Remaining powerfully poignant, war grave cemeteries are found in every nation where world war battles were fought. There are 23,000 worldwide. Each one tells the story of how nations come to terms with the unprecedented loss of life.

The headstones are lined up in perfect uniformity, but no words can prepare a visitor for the overwhelming sense of loss that still prevails within them.

Pixie Woodstock

Beneath The Silver Stars

I   A thousand crosses painted white,
beneath a greying sky.
Standing stark against the green-
no cause to wonder why.

II   The waxy blue of fallen flesh,
lays still beneath the mud.
Whilst buttercups with golden heads
reside in fields above.

III   The pink flushed faces of their loves,
still blush with youthful life.
Each tender gentle English rose,
each lover, child and wife.

IV   Whilst far away from England's soil,
they lay with battle scars.
In endless regimented rows,
beneath the silver stars.

Syria

I   World grown weary, lies are spun.
Texts are sent and favours won.

      Puppeteers who lust for power,
      they care not for their final hours.

III   In lies they deal, they covet dread,
the fears they shape within your head.

      Sabers rattle, missiles fly,
      death rains down as children die.

V   A promise made, we once stood tall,
for nations rise when good men fall.

      Mothers, daughters, fathers and sons,
      no more to wake and greet the sun.

VII   As days turn dark and shadows crawl,
perhaps a chance, one final call.

      Upon this ledge, misunderstood,
      a plea from those who trust in good.

IX   Take not a step that leads to war,
but turn towards a safer shore.

Stephan J Myers

---

x   Where men and women come around
      and find themselves on common ground.

          Where peace is praised and war we shun,
          this web of life was richly spun.

xii   A gift for all, to pass along,
      these moments ours to right a wrong.

          Let liberty and peace prevail
          and lift the shadow of war's veil.

"Proud to fight for England's Green.
Glory days, so it would seem."

Beyond the pomp and fervor of national
pride there is no glory in war. When
countries seek to settle their differences by
force parents will always bury sons and
daughters as futures wither on the vine.

Stephan J Myers

Conscription

I

We wave them off in search of glory.
Reality a different story.

Baby faced with fuzzy beards,
marching off to face their fears.

III

With shiny boots and ruddy faces,
Sergeant puts them through their paces.

Ripped apart from mother's breast.
Too immature to face this test.

V

Sweethearts pictures in their hands,
off they go to other lands.

Fueled with fervour, gum and fags.
Strangely fond of ID tags.

VII

Proud to fight for England's Green.
Glory days, so it would seem.

Until the mud and sweat and fear,
makes all the glory disappear.

IX

Rotting feet in trenches grim,
giving up would be a sin.

So chin up guys, and on they go.
Over the top to face the foe.

XI

Comrades lying bleeding, broke.
Tanks and guns go up in smoke.

Desperation all around.
Body parts strewn over ground.

XIII

Warfare gobbling up these lives,
making widows out of wives.

Mothers cry for missing sons-
this is how all war becomes.

XV

So minister consider first.
Imagine conflict at its worst.

Be bloody sure before you call,
these pure of heart to give their all.

"They took him off to save the world
A fragile man, so new unfurled."

When counting the casualties of war they must never be limited to the dead and the wounded.

War destroys lives with more souls becoming casualties of war than physical bodies, with none more vulnerable than those of mothers who have lost their children.

Pixie Woodstock

The Call Up

I

They took my son; my only boy.
They stole my life; my source of joy.
My memories of happy days,
of giggling mouths and funny ways.

They took the warmth of baby skin,
nestled there beneath my chin.
Of powdered bottoms, round and soft.
Of laughing faces, held aloft.

III

They took the joy of crafts, and arts.
Of sticky fingers making tarts.
And all the evenings reading books,
with drooping lids and loving looks.

The knobbly knees with scabs and scrapes,
and tellings-off for being late.
Returning home from school with news,
a slick of mud on shiny shoes.

V

They took his soft and downy curls,
which sat against his head in whorls.
His coltish legs, his cheeky grin.
The energy and life within.

They took his manhood, newly formed.
The breaking voice, now much transformed.
My handsome boy turned seventeen.
The years much treasured, in between.

VII

They took him off to save the world,
a fragile man, so new unfurled.
Just to borrow, so they said,
but now my boy lies cold and dead.

No memory is safe from grief,
his life a whisper, all too brief.
They stole my life, my source of joy.
They took my son; my only boy.

"Let marching bands proclaim the hour.
Lay woven wreaths and wear your flower."

From 1914 to 1918, World War I took a greater human toll than any previous conflict, with some 8.5 million soldiers dead of battlefield injuries or disease.

When Lieutenant Colonel John McCrae, a Canadian who served as a brigade surgeon for an Allied artillery unit, spotted a cluster of poppies shortly after the Second Battle of Ypres, he was so struck by the sight of the bright red blooms amongst the carnage of battle that he wrote his iconic poem, "In Flanders Field," in which he channeled the voice of the fallen soldiers buried under those hardy poppies.

If our fallen could speak would they say we have truly honoured their sacrifice?

Pixie Woodstock

Poppy Day

I

A vivid dream, too bright to last.
With acrid smoke soon overcast.
No more to dream, I said, no more.
On memories I've come to soar.

II

A thousand youthful souls there slain,
and I then one with death's cold chain.
Cast from entrails blood and gore,
and lost to life for ever more.

III

A thousand men each sound of mind,
and I amongst them now enshrined.
A simple cross above my grave,
recalls the life I freely gave.

IV

Don't mar this moment, solemn, still.
Don't dwell on loss and bare no ill.
Let marching bands proclaim the hour.
Lay woven wreaths and wear your flower.

V

Forget me not, don't think to brood.
Don't dwell upon my solitude.
These fields from which you slowly turn,
stand testament so hearts might learn.

VI

My vivid dream, too bright to last,
with men's dark deeds soon overcast.
Be sure I harboured no regret.
Just pledge to me you'll not forget.

"Once more to soar where eagles dare.
As tracers bright cut swathes through air."

When Winston Churchill said "Never in the field of human conflict was so much owed by so many to so few", he was paying tribute to the enormous efforts made by fighter pilots and bomber crews to establish air superiority.

The skies were a dangerous place to be during World War II and nothing made a fighter pilot more aware of his limitations than bailing out of a plane consumed by fire as it plummeted towards the earth. It took incredible courage to return to the skies again.

Stephen J Myers

Where Eagles Dare

A falling star through black of night,
illumed by tracer burning bright.
A man apart I bank and wheel,
ensconced within my frame of steel.

Addicted to the thrill of flight,
to climb and dive in dogged fight.
Amidst the sanctuary of cloud.
with canon loosed and engine loud.

III

Fleet of wing 'neath Heaven's veil,
this bird of prey from which I fell.
A downward rush a brush with death.
Night's frigid air, a fight for breath.

My chute unfurls, once more to rise,
as flames ignite before my eyes.
A puppet pulled by silken strings,
as all around me banshees sing.

Stephan J Myers

V

A momentary lapse of time.
A player in a mummer's mime.
A wave of heat engulfing me.
The wings of death I clearly see.

My comrades plunging from the sky,
just men like me and born to fly.
Men who called the heavens home,
through which their souls will surely roam.

VI

The hands of time now spinning fast.
I know this jump won't be my last.
With lag pursuit, inverted spin,
I'll pull back yoke and join my kin.

Once more to soar where eagles dare,
as tracers bright cut swathes through air.
A fighter jock I'll duel with death,
till combat takes my final breath.

"A fight to stem the tears and grief.
The pain of loss, of shared belief."

Language, culture and religion remain the greatest barriers to peace with war a damning manifestation of their divide. And yet war does not determine who is right, only who, through might, prevails.

No matter how necessary or justified war seems there is only one inescapable fact that comes from it. That only the dead have seen the end of war.

Stephen J Myers

Ukraine

I

A world of wars,
A war of worlds.
Divided lands
with flags unfurled.

A fight for borders
firmly drawn.
While territories
crash and burn.

III

A fight for air,
for land and sea.
While people die
or fight or flee.

A fight of life
with shattered breath.
As bombs explode;
the hunt of death.

V

A fight for freedom,
march of boots.
Of trucks and tanks
and guns that shoot.

A fight to catch
the last exhale.
To staunch the blood
as flesh grows pale.

VII

A fight to stem
the tears and grief.
The pain of loss,
of shared belief.

A fight before
all life's release.
A fight to keep
the world at peace.

*"Silence shattered, whistles blow,
and over we must go."*

In the grit and grime of the trenches men drowned in shell-holes already filled with decaying flesh as the bullets flew around them. In them soldiers came to know the true meaning of despair, death and fear as they found themselves cast into an abyss of sorrow.

But going 'over the top', to climb out of their trenches, carrying their weapons as they ran through the enemy's 'field of fire' over complex labyrinths of barbed wire, was to dance with the devil himself.

Stephen J Myers

The Trench

I   A bloom of white against the night.
Fragile breath, too weak to fight.
Weary frame, flesh hanging slack.
Tendons seizing, fighting back.

II   Ligaments stretched tight with fright.
Rigid muscles, poised for flight.
Putrid feet in rotting boots.
Hands froze hard in mock salute.

III   Brittle bones in freezing sludge.
Faces smeared with fear and mud.
Rats run wild from bed to bed,
feasting on the fallen dead.

IV   A bloom of white against the night,
with dove like wings it takes to flight.
Stark against the inky black,
where other soldiers watch their back.

V   A whispered murmur now outrun.
A soldier grimly cocks his gun.
He sets his sights and takes his aim,
trained for warfare-trained to maim.

VI   Beneath the camouflage of dark
the shot rings cleanly, loud and stark.
Two feet below the freezing breath,
a body slumps towards its death.

VII   A bloom of white against the night,
the faintest life force taking flight.
That one exhale a heavy price,
a shrunken frame betrayed by life.

VIII   A body wallows in the mud,
as rats come quick to sup the blood.
Their hungry teeth to tear and feast,
no conscious thought in sweet release.

IX   Someone's Husband, Father, Son.
Nothing left when war is done.
The shocking truth of strife and greed,
to fill a politicians need.

Statues In The Fog

I   Statues crouch in freezing fog,
       stony cold in fading light.
           Haunted ears stretched wide with fear.
           Silence screams into the night.

II   No man's land a hallowed stretch,
       separating men from fate.
           Before the final desperate dash,
           a breathless terrifying wait.

III   Eyes shut tight in frozen fear,
       waiting for the call of death.
           Bayonets clutched closer still,
           witnesses to sobbing breath.

IV   Liquid legs refuse the shout,
       buckled under sagging knees.
           Strength of youth dissolved in dread-
           prayers fly high in hopeless pleas.

V   Barely grown with tender minds,
       each a soul of precious worth.
           Strewn in death on no man's land.
           Sacrificed for Mother Earth.

Without Remorse

Barbs of death before me
twisted cruel without remorse.
Manifest from darkest minds
and I must run this course.

II

Brothers stand below me,
grim and still on splintered rungs.
Steadfast breath and resolute,
our race with death begun.

III

Silence shattered, whistles blow,
and over we must go.
A symphony of death,
we race towards our foe.

IV

I stagger, stumble, rise again,
cordite stings my eyes.
Ears are ringing, muffled screams,
as one by one we die.

V

A ragged run, guns held tight,
as shells burst all around.
No dignity in death's embrace.
Bodies on the ground.

VI

Strong of limb and stout of heart,
each turned to ashen grey.
Dead and gone, their race now run,
amidst this hellish fray.

VII

I pull my trigger, fill my lungs,
crazed without remorse.
Battle forged in Hell's domain,
committed to this course.

"Your body fell, your spark long gone, your gift to me still lingers on."

War does not begin and end the way we think it does. It begins with the belief in freedom nurtured by the sacrifices of our fallen. With their willingness to face their darkest fears so that those for whom they fought can face their tomorrows without ever knowing the full extent of the sacrifices they made.

Stephan J Myers

The Fallen

Your picture hung upon the wall,
an easy smile, proud and tall.

A hand me down from days of glory,
a distant time, a soldier's story.

On foreign shores you closed your eyes,
a life you gave, no mournful sigh.

Duty bound, a call to heed,
your sacrifice your greatest deed.

V

A moment known to none but you,
your courage held, your heart stayed true.

Your name unheard, your face unseen,
I stand to pray in pastures green.

I take a breath and tears I shed,
I open eyes to fields of red.

On errant breeze a soulful sigh,
I hear your name, an anguished cry.

IX

Your body fell, your spark long gone,
your gift to me still lingers on.

No coin paid, no payment due,
a sunny day with sky of blue.

So many days I woke to sun,
a life to live, to eat and run.

For days go quick, no time to waste,
you wait for me in all my haste.

XIII

I lived a life for you and I,
no pithy lows, I sought the highs.

Those moments clear, when all is known,
a body strong, a child now grown.

These shoulders broad, a debt now due,
my path is set, my thoughts of you.

A life and choices soon to make,
a spirit free, a step to take.

XVII

I think of you and all you saw,
I wonder if you wished for more.

Each moment lost that turned to days,
so many years they fade away.

I stood to wait upon our wall,
I heard the cheers that hailed the fall.

I looked for you as crowds walked by,
upon my toes, my neck held high.

XXI

So many danced, laughed and sung.
Dark days past, the new begun.

I thought about our last goodbye.
I wiped the tears that stung my eyes.

Cap in hand, a cheery smile,
you stood beyond the gate a while.

I saw you turn and wave to me,
the tears I cried you could not see.

XXV

A smile upon my face you saw,
a hand held high and nothing more.

I read the papers every day,
before I slept I knelt to pray.

I said a prayer and wondered why,
so many fathers had to die?

So far away, no one to hold,
no loved ones near when all turns cold.

XXIX

A moment past, a spirit flown,
last words lost, your thoughts unknown.

At last a knock upon our door,
hollow words and nothing more.

At school they laughed and called me names,
they left me out when playing games.

I balled my fists and stood my ground,
I took it all without a sound.

XXXIII

You taught me well and tall I stood,
I sought in all the spark of good.

A kiss upon my lips recalled,
a fluttering heart I quickly walled.

Memories now, in dark of night,
loves long lost and out of sight.

I take a step, all fear has fled.
I think of all the books I read.

XXXVII

Of love and honour, quests for gold,
tall tales new and those of old.

Talk of heroes bold and brave,
sacrifices each one gave.

I read of places far away,
of freedom lost and darkest days.

Of fearless souls who heard the bell,
a solemn toll for those who fell.

XLI

I wonder who you stood beside,
standing tall, no thought to hide.

All for one and one for all,
to stand and fight, to rise and fall.

I think of all held near and dear,
thoughts betray my darkest fear.

That I might fail to stand my ground
and make my peace without a sound.

XLV

This heart that beats within my
chest, I wonder will it come to rest?

Upon this day, on foreign shores,
what right have I to ask for more?

The sound of war is all around,
but in our ranks we make no sound.

The fated ones, no jests we make,
our hearts are stout, no troths we break.

XLIX

For love of life and those held dear,
we stand to fight, our purpose clear.

Of lovers fair and babes in arms,
we pray we keep them safe from harm.

If this must be our final call,
stay close and lift me when I fall.

You and I, we are as one,
a father lost, a loving son.

LIII

Carry me, to heights on high,
where I can say my last goodbye.

I feel the pride that made you strong,
the flame that burns to right a wrong.

The spark that lives inside us all,
that burns most bright when duty calls.

At last the sound of distant guns,
a new day's dawn, an end begun.

LVII

I make my peace, all fear has fled,
I think of pastures green not red.

I see your picture on our wall,
an easy smile proud and tall.

I lace my boots, I take my gun,
I walk towards the setting sun.

Original pastel artwork for The
Fallen by Stephan J Myers.

A Soldier Lost

I   Once upon a dark night fair,

           I SOLDIERED LOST WITHOUT A CARE.

II   War born phantoms all abound,
           their presence felt in all around.

III   Sounds to stoke my darkest fears.
           On wind their whispers reached my ears,

IV   I'd fought the fight and honour kept,
           for friends I'd lost, I prayed and wept.

V   Once upon a dark night fair,

           I WANDERED LOST WITHOUT A CARE.

∞

War

I   **_War!_**

          Bells are rung, to silent fall.
          Presses run, out goes the call.

          Across the land, to young and old.
          Drums to beat as tales are told.

II   **_War!_**

          Foreign fields, strange sounding names.
          Battle lines in rich men's games.

          Seduced are we by honeyed lies.
          To rise and fall 'neath distant skies.

III   **_War!_**

          Fathers, brothers, uncles, sons.
          Each one proud to lug their gun.

          Soldiers all with happy smiles.
          Hob nail boots eat up the miles.

IV **_War!_**

> Soon enough they`re at the front.
> Shoulders braced they take the brunt.
>
> Swathes of lead, a haunting sight.
> Cut them down in dead of night.

V **War!**

> Shattered minds and body parts.
> Piled up high on horse drawn carts.
>
> No pealing bells to hail their fall.
> Just faceless names on village walls.

VI **War!**

> Days and weeks they turn to years.
> The dead lay cold and yet we cheer.
>
> Celebrating victories won,
> as mothers mourn their fated sons.

The following poem is dedicated to the
memory of Trooper James 'Magpie' Munday
KIA 15.10.08 Marjah Afghanistan.

We Fall As One

I Molten metal, shards of death,
this acrid smell that taints our breath.

No loud applause, no golden light.
Just blood and guts in dark of night.

III He glances quick with startled eyes.
No sound he makes, no haunting sighs.

I sense the lurch and halt of heart,
the end of life and death's cold start.

V Together now in silence bound,
I dare not move or make a sound.

We stood together, fought as one.
We talked of daughters, wives and sons.

VII Of choices made that brought us here.
The lives we lived and things held dear.

Now blood runs red as rivulets run.
The night turns cold no warmth of sun.

IX Two errant boys, as men we fought.
For Queen and country freedom sought.

x   Schooled in war we faced our fears.
We made our choice, no need for tears.

I hear them now as close they come.
My body weak. my legs turned numb.

xii   Blood congealed on arid sand,
my brother lost I make my stand.

Of death's restraints I have no fear.
I feel his lingering presence near.

xiv   Proud to soldier, duty done.
Together now, we fall as one.

The following poem is dedicated to the memory
of Warrant Officer L. E. Cavill.

Sgt. SLAUGHTER

I   **Sergeant Slaughter, hear my cry.**
As all around me bullets fly.

Hunkered down 'neath leaden sky.
I watch as good men rise to die.

Soft and stout with eyes of green.
I came to you, no war I'd seen.

You cared not for the boy I'd been.
You ran us hard and made us lean.

II   **Sergeant Slaughter schooled in war.**
We stood before you each in awe.

We took our oaths to duty do.
For Queen and country blood runs true.

With reddened face and lips turned blue,
you made us crawl through shite for you.

You shook us early from our racks,
to break our backs with weighted packs.

III   ***Sergeant Slaughter man of steel.***
You coaxed us on with boot and heel.

Your devil dogs on icy tracks,
we dug in deep with spade and axe.

As one by one we fell away,
so fewer woke to face each day.

You tried to break us one and all,
on wind swept moors from spring to fall.

IV   ***Sergeant Slaughter head held high.***
You never said we trained to die.

You gave us guns, you said take aim.
We learnt to kill, to rend and maim.

But cardboard cutouts don't fight back,
don't feign defeat or press attack.

Now last light fades and tracer flies,
the kiss of death and our demise.

V **Sergeant Slaughter quick to curse.**
Caustic, cutting, always terse.

You called us names and put us down,
but spoke with pride of Queen and crown.

By God's good grace you made us men.
We learned to fall and rise again.

But boys no more and off to war,
I wonder what in us you saw.

VI **Sergeant Slaughter standing tall.**
Quick to rise and last to fall.

We followed you and held our ground.
No protest made, no errant sound.

A prouder man I could not be,
to know you fought and fell with me.

7/5/1945

My Darling Dorothea

When I first met you, I yet did not know my destiny.
A laughing, bright-eyed girl you were.
Filled with the bubbles of life and zestful in the living of it.
The sparkling in your eyes, the quickness of your smile.
And the young force which surged through you in seeming waves.
Gave my mind a disquiet which made me shrink from you.
More slowly than the bud unfolding.
Did I learn the secrets of you.
Hidden behind the sparkling eyes and laughing lips,
The shapely form and comely face.
The grace and the appealing charm of you.
Which was shown to my eyes.

      - When I first met you.
        I love you precious -
        your prosaic but not very
        prossey husband, *Bob*

The Following poem is dedicated to the memory of
Lieut. Horace Robert Walter Tayler & Dorothea
Falconer Tayler.

65

Silent Echoes

I   A soldier is never forgotten.
He lives in the hearts he has left.
His steps will be ever remembered,
in minds of the sad and bereft.

II   He walks in the steps of his children,
remains warm in the arms of his wife.
Stays wrapped in the comfort of parents,
who cherished his blossoming life.

III   His breath felt in blustery mornings.
His joy in the heat of the sun.
His tears in the wonder of rainfall,
as his leaves dropped to earth, one by one.

IV   Recollected in moments of silence-
in the bustle of family life.
As flowers are laid at his graveside,
by his ever remembering wife.

Remembrance

I   Do not a silent vigil keep,
I have no need of dreams or sleep.
Upon the winds that gently blow,
my spirit free from all below.

    Recall my face in summer's sun,
on sultry nights that once held fun.
Where Eden ran, its waters deep,
a secret place not ours to keep.

III   Look for me in autumn's rain,
in sun's first kiss where silence reigns.
As daylight breaks no need to rush,
I linger still in dawn's sweet hush.

    As winter's crown falls all around,
when nights are long and clocks rewound.
Dream of me when warmth you seek,
on darkest days when all looks bleak.

V   Think of me when spring has sprung,
when shoots are green and songs are sung.
Let thoughts of sadness wane and fade
for love is cruel, a jagged blade.

VI   Your vigil past, our story spun,
     we ran our race, we loved and won.
     Cherished thoughts of days now past,
     for seasons change and nothing lasts.

          Laugh and sing, embrace your days,
          the moon's caress and morning's blaze.
          No more the drums that herald war,
          a nation's hopes of bloodless shores.

"Ignorant of sunken souls,
where battles rage and futures fade."

The time to tally the cost of war is before the first shot is fired. The cost of every life lost upon the battlefield, every widow, every orphan, every lover, every friend.

A debt that can never be repaid and yet so easily incurred by politicians more often than not divorced from a lifetime debt of loss.

Stephan J Myers

I Solemnly Declare

I   No recourse, heatedly committed,
a new just war declared.

> Virtuous in their declarations,
> a nation's fangs are bared.

III   By those who won the popular vote,
their deeds they will enshrine.

> What thoughts give they to those who'll fall,
> to your families and mine?

V   With each new day the presses run,
our fears so hurriedly fed.

> Our hearts and minds their passions fanned,
> desire for war quick bred.

VII   Opinions shared by learned tongues,
do diligently proclaim.

> The last war fought, forgotten now,
> along with it our shame.

Stephan J Myers

IX Our troops we laud, cheer with pride,
across this land and hereabout.

        Feelings high and overwrought,
        we're quick to swear and gamely shout.

XI Their bounteous youth, their vibrant dreams,
the promises we made.

        Ignorant of sunken souls,
        where battles rage and futures fade.

XIII And when at last their duty done
and homeward are they bound.

        We are quick to spurn their point of view,
        and scarcely make a sound.

XV Disgraced are we, our liberty bought,
war's sorrows must be borne.

        Not by men who gave their all,
        but the pledges we have sworn.

"I have no words with you to share.
For drenched in death my words have fled."

In bygone wars before the internet soldiers in the field often had little or no contact with home while on duty and letters from home gave them the connection that they lost.

In 1945 alone, nearly three billion pieces of mail were exchanged between service members, friends and family with mail call being one of the most cherished rituals of soldiers and sailors in combat. And yet sometimes the vast differences between home life and war at the front created a chasm between soldiers and their families which was hard to breach and soldiers would find it increasingly difficult to write.

Stephan J Myers

No words Have I

I

My love,
send no more letters please.
I've read the news
and heard men talk.
Of why we must stand stout and strong.

II

I've watched
as planes fly overhead.
Missiles pounding
enemy lines.
And have no thoughts of right and wrong.

III

Your words
that tell of joy and fears.
Will never change
the tides of war.
Where battles waged will linger long.

IV

I have no words
with you to share.
For drenched in death
my words have fled.
But know that here I now belong.

V

A soldier, weary,
bruised and torn.
Deprived of sleep
and oft forlorn.
But home amongst this maddened throng.

We...

I

We rest but listless get no sleep.

We rise to meet each dawning day.

We laugh aloud and often weep.

To soldier all our cares away.

We are the sons of circumstance.

We bleed for every bough we gain.

We give ourselves to luck and chance.

To languish in the arms of pain.

Paladin

Forged cold in war this heart of stone.
No tenderness or beauty known.

A paladin of liberty.
So you unburdened might walk free.

Your angel's face once lit my smile.
Not long, but for a little while.

A fleeting tryst beneath the stars.
My heart now caged by leaden bars.

V

This fodder dark on which I feed.
Cares not for blooms yet leaves its seed.

A dark and twisted marish gray.
That seeks to crush the light of day.

All hope now lost no songs to sing.
I dread what break of dawn will bring.

A tremulous sigh my prayers unsaid.
For words will never raise the dead.

Aftermath

I   Missing moments, terrors untold,
phantom friends I knew so well.

II   Merciless, haunting, no kind respite,
this hell in which I dwell.

III   Deaths dark wraiths stalk all my days,
beyond your will to understand.

IV   Freedom, the drug our sanity bought,
you sit and hold my hand.

V   My duty done, I wear this mask,
for the guilt you cannot see.

VI   A stranger here, I have come to pray
for death to set me free.

*"Restless soldier drifting by
on westward winds I hear you sigh."*

The Menin Gate memorial in Belgium commemorates 54,896 missing Allied combatants who are known to have been killed in the Ypres Salient. The Douaumont ossuary, meanwhile, contains 130,000 unidentifiable sets of French and German remains from the Battle of Verdun. In the United States Armed Forces, 78,750 personnel missing in action had been reported by the end of the war, representing over 19 percent of the total of 405,399 killed during the conflict.

The numbers are staggering but perhaps the greatest tragedy were the lives lived in the knowledge loved ones could never be laid to rest. For some it was simply overwhelming.

Homeward Bound was written for the wife of a soldier missing in action who finally came to take her own life. Her reflections taken from letters found after her death.

Stephan J Myers

Homeward Bound

I

I glimpse your ghost about there,
fore westward winds and brine tinged air.

Where the waves they break on golden sands,
that spot on which you'd stand.

III

I heard the wistful words you spoke;
homeward bound, a promise broke.

And prayed that heavenly clouds would part
and I could brace your heart.

V

Truest love, no grave for you,
no mound or cross to mournful rue.

War's shattered promises enshrined,
to the past they're now consigned.

IV

Restless soldier drifting by
on westward winds I hear you sigh.

Where the waves they break on golden sands,
that's where I'll always stand.

IX

Would that I could reach you there,
beyond the pale of life's rich fare.

Where angels stand fore heaven's gates,
where last we'll know our fates.

XI

I'd hold you close your eyes to seek,
still your lips lest you should speak.

For words mean naught when love prevails,
our heavenly souls to sail.

XIII

Dearest love now free of pain,
on westward winds we'll wax and wane.

Where the waves they break on golden sands,
together then we'll stand.

XV

On sun kissed days when daisies grow,
you and I such peace shall know.

Far from those dreaded fields of flame,
where they'll never know your name.

XVII

My restless soldier long now dead,
not for you those fields of red.

Just westward winds fore brine tinged air,
you and I, our ghosts now there.

"I saw the twisted limbs stained bright with blood."

Far too often we see the aftermath of war. Caught in glimpses and hurriedly turned away from because we're unsure how we should react.

Perhaps it's the guilt we feel when coming face to face with the reality of a sacrifice another has made to ensure our freedom?

Stephan J Myers

The Soldier

I caught his eye when looking down at vegetables.
The supermarket heaving,
full of flustered Mums with crying kids who ran
amok between the isles,
and long limbed ladies clipping on stiletto heels.

He had no legs to run, or clip, or even walk.
His face dead level with the middle shelf
as people passed and stretched above him,
wafts of heady scent and body odour
falling down in tiny droplets
settling in ignorance among his springing curls.

His eyes were green-and startling.
Eyes that no-one saw,
save perhaps the quieter children
pulled along by rushing Dads,
who stopped in momentary wonder at the man
who had no legs-and just one arm.

But on that solitary arm his muscles rippled,
tightly coddled by the flimsy cloth.
The strength of twenty men lay there in wait.
Strength and grim determination
drowning and eclipsing all the ladies clipping on
stiletto heels,
the flustered able bodied Mums and rushing Dads
and running kids.

And as I looked into his eyes I saw the former soldier,
straight and strong,
with lithe limbs loosely bouncing as he jogged between
the sandy hills,
full of life and young and whole.

A photograph against his breast, secreted snugly there
against his heart,
which twenty minutes later ceased to beat, as others,
ashen faced as him had pounded fiercely,
both with fists and will, to fire it's leaden deadness
once again with life.

I saw the twisted limbs stained bright with blood,
which pumped between the blackened flesh.
So stark against the gauze of medics vainly staunching
endless crimson rivers flowing freely from his heart;
the salty tears which chased a sticky path
between the dusty half congealing blood to soak the
springing curls.

I saw the pain of loss and grief and agony, an etching
gouged across his twisted face.
Each moment after lived upon that knife edge,
slippery and steep on either side,
each willing him to fall into their waiting arms.

Whispering and murmuring and offering oblivion in
pills or at the bottom of a bottle.
Faces drooping, grey and sad with sympathy,
his missing limbs more relevant than any flesh
they left behind.

But pulling back, I met his gaze;
a twinkle in the startling eyes, a free and easy smile.
Vitality and health eclipsing all the ladies
clipping on stiletto heels, the flustered Mums and
rushing Dads and running kids.

I saw the essence of a man unchanged, as strong and
lithe and whole as ever,
lifting up his last remaining hand and running
sunburned fingers through a head of springing curls.

"They talk in whispers, faces grey.
Tell me why they look that way."

How do you tell a child that their father
or mother's sacrifice is a silent grief they
must bear throughout their life. That
their last image of them must suffice for
a lifetime?

Stephan J Myers

Mummy Dear

I

Mummy, where has daddy gone?
He's been away for far too long.

He used to tuck me up in bed,
but now it's always you instead.

III

Mummy dear, have I been bad?
Your eyes are always sad.

You say that daddy's doing fine,
and will return to us in time.

V

Mummy, why is grandma here?
Why did she come to hold you near?

Why did you go out wearing black,
and when is daddy coming back?

VII

Mummy, now your shoulders droop.
The neighbours come round bringing soup.

They talk in whispers, faces grey.
Tell me why they look that way.

IX

Mummy tell me why you cry,
and say that daddy's in the sky.

We know that daddy's doing fine,
and will return to us in time.

Identity Tags

Torn from you, tags cold and grey,
no memories held within.

Yet in my palm I feel you close,
hot breath and stubble chin.

I see the one I came to love,
my world, my life, my whole.

Wayward warrior, tender kind,
with selfless giving soul.

V

You fought for us, our liberty,
free will, our right to choose.

A soldier forged on war torn lands
with everything to lose.

We never talked about this day,
of reaper gave no heed.

Now all I have are ID Tags
and platitudes to read.

Lament Me Not

I

My time grows short, my limbs grow weak.
The darkness calls where there I'll seek.

Where questions that have plagued my mind,
their answers I must surely find.

I take a breath, my chest feels tight,
no more the strength to stand and fight.

Leaden legs betray me now,
and so I take my final bow.

V

I fought the fight, for freedom fell.
Don't sing my name or ring the bell.

A man who rightly feared his death,
with pounding heart and ragged breath.

I cared not for the praise death brings,
for fall did I for grander things.

*"She offers up a voiceless scream.
The silence caught against her palm."*

The casualties of war are not limited to the dead and the wounded, for more wives and mothers become casualties of war than those who fall.

Stephan J Myers

The Telegram

I

The day is warm, with gentle breeze,
which carries voices clear and young.

From where they play on cobbled street,
their laughter bright with joyous fun.

III

It eddies round the nets, which skip.
Their dance revealing summer's haze.

Which beckons eyes to look beyond,
at nature's gifts, with grateful gaze.

V

The babbling child neath dappled leaves,
which faintly stir in bluest skies.

His chubby legs burned berry brown.
With mother's smile and father's eyes.

VII

The grass is moist beneath her feet.
The nappies billow on the line.

The faintest buzz of busy bees,
between the foxgloves there to dine.

IX

She lifts her face to court the warmth,
her senses sated, full of bliss.

As England's glory soaks her skin-
what finer land is there than this?

XI

She passes by the cooing child,
a smile upon her perfect lips.

With swinging steps towards the house,
the basket balanced on her hip.

XIII

But as she steps from light to dark,
a chill assaults her toasted skin.

The recesses inside her mind,
allow the fear to rush within.

XV

The street turned quiet, she hears his tread.
She wills his steps to walk on by.

A dirge already beating time,
to bury joy, and hope deny.

XVII

As rooted to that place she stands,
he passes through the creaking gate.

His shadow creeps beneath the door,
with greedy hands to seal her fate.

XIX

She offers up a voiceless scream,
the silence caught against her palm.

To shatter upward through her mind,
her eyes stretched wide in mute alarm.

XXI

And all the while the gurgling child,
smiles blithely up toward his mum.

Innocently unaware,
that he will be an only son.

"Embracing hell with blood streaked face,
to slither, crawl, with death to race."

In WW-I stretcher-bearers experienced life and death on battlefields unlike any others in history, coming under fire from shells and gas canisters as they waded through mud or shell craters to move men away from the worst of the battle.

In many instances, they would carry a casualty through enemy fire only to find that when they finally got to an aid station or ambulance he was dead. Sometimes they fell before they reached the safety of their front line.

Stephan J Myers

Angel In The Dark

I

This flag's not his, yet now he stands
amidst this cold and war torn land.
    A foreigner whose conscience bade
    a sacrifice he freely gave.

II

No gun to hold or bullets fire
yet stand he did amongst the mire.
    Broken bodies wrought asunder
    skyline rent with manmade thunder.

III

The smell of earth that's seeped in blood
a trickle first and now a flood.
    To hear the cries as comrades fall,
    Valhalla's heroes one and all.

IV

His legs were weak yet quick to stand,
no gun but stretcher in his hand.
    He thought not of the steps he'd take,
    the tempting target that he'd make.

—— » ——

V

Through acrid dust with blood shot eyes
but drawn to those who mournful cry.
      I see him now recall his name
      the one not called who freely came.

VI

Embracing hell with blood streaked face,
to slither, crawl, with death to race.
      No count we kept as lives he saved,
      the paths for futures that he paved.

VII

The broken risen, lives to lead,
our victor over death's dark deed.
      And when I fell for fall I did,
      he ran to me whilst others hid.

VIII

His stretcher lost, his labored breath
and I upon the brink of death.
      Just flashes now but still he's near,
      recall his strength and lack of fear.

IX

His shoulders broad, each ragged breath,
to lift me from the jaws of death.
   His legs beneath us wavered not,
   till last a fatal bullet shot.

X

I felt the ice cold rush of death,
the blood and spittle from his breath.
   And yet a hundred more steps ran.
   A feat beyond mere mortal man.

XI

Below our flag he came to stand,
amidst this bloodied war torn land.
   My angel with his dirty face.
   For me he ran his final race.

Florence

It's quiet now- the midnight hour.
Sweet ether calms the soldiers cries.

> Save rustling silk of petticoats.
> A deathly hush 'neath canvas skies.

She glides between them, lamp held high,
through rows and rows of endless pain.

> At childish cheeks stained perfect pink,
> a lullaby their last refrain.

A stolen moment gone too fast,
death's rattle greets the dawning day.

> Another child is lost to war.
> His future crushed amongst the fray.

"His iron grave beneath the waves,
his name in stone to stay."

On 14 October 1939, Royal Oak was anchored at Scapa Flow in Orkney, Scotland, when she was torpedoed by the German submarine U-47. Of Royal Oak's complement of 1,234 men and boys, 835 were killed that night or died later of their wounds. The wreck of Royal Oak, a designated war grave, lies almost upside down in 100 feet (30 m) of water with her hull 16 feet (4.9 m) beneath the surface. In an annual ceremony marking the loss of the ship, Royal Navy divers place a White Ensign flag underwater at her stern.

Amongst those who lost their lives was Charles E Eyres, Boy Signalman, P/JX 155943, MPK

Stephan J Myers

An Ode To Charlie Eyres

The fated fallen lost to life,
a boy not yet a man.
Within the silent waters drift,
the ashes of his grandest plan.

Beneath grey Scarpa flow so deep,
a dark and endless sleep.
Where technicoloured dreams once dared,
now turned to dust as others weep.

III

No thoughts had he of silent men,
as wistfully he slept.
Whose company he'd come to keep,
as death upon him stealthy crept.

Predator in dark of night,
a fire quick to burn.
Cruel disregard for lives unlived
as war's conventions overturn.

V

His iron grave beneath the waves,
his name in stone to stay.
No modicum of joy for him,
remembered now as others pray.

Denied the melody of life,
of snow on moonlit streets.
The warmth of sultry kisses shared,
as passions flare to backstreet beats.

VII

The much tramped leaves of autumn's fall,
the whirl of winds subdued.
No chaste embrace as love takes hold
and promise leads to vows renewed.

No bells to toll, no ring to give,
where comfort surely lies.
No fireside at end of day,
no tears of joy and sparkling eyes.

IX

An endless winter, fathoms deep,
records his memory.
No pastures green, no fleeting words,
'neath dappled leaves on masonry.

No woeful march to times decay,
no more of war's distain.
No years to grieve for all things lost
the lives and dreams of brothers slain.

XI

For Charlie just a single rose,
and barely seventeen.
Lest we forget the dreams he had,
the life he gave and peace unseen.

Charlie Eyres

Objection

I   His gaze is firm, his shoulders tall.
His legs stand wide, lest he should fall.

    The smell of leather, creaking chairs.
Disgusted looks, reproachful stares.

III   Dust stinging nostrils, smarting eyes,
with sweating palms, no-where to hide.

    They bring the book and make him swear,
though his convictions lie in there.

V   With grave expressions they begin,
not understanding, they won't win.

    Steeped in glory, one and all,
they rise to fight and fight to fall.

VII   His faith revealing all they lack,
their cannon fodder fighting back.

    They make their case, he makes his own—
the stand he takes is his alone.

IX   His principles come shining through.
He will not kill what 'ere they do.

They bind him tightly, find their sights,
his soul unscathed by mortal blight.

XI   They rise to shoot, he falls apart,
a comrades bullet through his heart.

But what about the enemy,
who come to maim and kill with glee?

XIII   And what of mother, wife and son.
Where will they be when war is done?

If Hitler wins where will we be?
Pray God will save humanity.

"This is not you, this man returned.
Replete with many medals earned."

Wars begin in the mind and in those
minds, love and compassion are quickly
walled lest the horrors that await
destroy the very things a soldier fights
for. It is little wonder then that few
return the same.

Stephan J Myers

Lost Love

I   This is not you, this man returned,
replete with many medals earned.

This soldier's step is not as sure.
His steps drag heavy on the floor.

III   Although your eyes are green and clear,
no depth remains as I come near.

You say you love me, draw me close,
but still I miss my lover's ghost.

V   The man my heart would call its own,
is left behind, I stand alone.

Encircled in his wraithlike arms,
embracing not my lover's charms.

VII   This sham, this shell, before my eyes,
is nothing that I recognize.

I yearn to feel our passion shared,
where dreams are made and souls are bared.

IX   I miss my love, his touch, his smell,
that crooked smile I know so well.

This haunted man is not like he,
who cared, and loved and cherished me.

XI   This thief called war, who stole my life,
who promised to a soldier's wife,

that he would bring security,
becomes instead my enemy.

The Fear Inside

I   At last I stand your love returned,
replete with many medals earned.

This soldier warped by war for sure.
His heart weighed down by blood and gore.

III   You tilt your head as I come near,
to meet green eyes that mask my fear.

You say you love me, hold me tight,
but do you sense what's out of sight?

V   A man bereft who stands alone,
who knows no peace to call his own.

Encircled in your cherished arms,
yet far removed from loves fair charms.

VII   This hollowed husk before your eyes,
is not a man I recognize.

I yearn to feel and passion share,
but harbor terrors not to share.

IX   I missed you love. Your touch, your smell,
that carefree smile I knew so well.

My love who vowed to stand by me.
This tortured soul is not like he.

XI   Your lover, soldier, nation's pride,
now dreads to show what writhes inside.

This thing called war may steal our life,
my precious darling soldier's wife.

"I cannot now, recall your smile.
My head is filled with all things vile."

It is not only the living who are killed in war. It is cruel and none can make it gentle. So we must count the cost not just in the tragedy of lives lost but also in the veterans who carry the burden of all they have seen.

Stephan J Myers

My Heart

I   My dear, my love, my sweet, my heart.
What madness caused our souls to part?

> My world, my stars, my moon, my sun,
> we two were made to be as one.

III   My heart lies heavy at my breast,
as weary, I lay down to rest.

> Your lips brush softly mine, I feel.
> In dreamlike state your touch is real.

V   I drink you in, your scent, your hair,
but wake to find no lover there.

> No limbs entwined nor mingled breath.
> Instead each day I face my death.

VII   Adoring eyes which dance and shine,
are fading fast within my mind.

> I cannot now, recall your smile.
> My head is filled with all things vile.

IX   Flushed pink from love, your silken skin,
now disappears amongst my sin.

     The gentle contours of your frame,
are camouflaged by guilt and shame.

XI   I crave the comfort of my wife,
amongst the screams of ending life.

     But as I slaughter, wound and maim,
I know we'll never be the same.

The Bands Play On

I Time relentless since we met,
   the briefest of affairs.

   Thousands jostling, minging wet,
   and us without a care.

III Time relentless war declared,
   I rose, I fell, I bled.

   The fiercest flames that burnt so bright,
   now lay cold and dead.

IV Time relentless whittling minds,
   dark terrors must I hide.

   The Bands play on, the Tors still wet,
   another by your side.

Just A Man

I **You think I do not mourn the dead,**
or those who by my hand have bled.
>You think I do not mourn their loss,
>the great divide I bade them cross.
>You think to take a life away,
>is but a game that soldiers play.
>You think I'm callous, cold inside,
>and from my actions quick to hide.

III To pull a trigger, not to see,
the lives destroyed in front of me.
>To pull a trigger, kill a man
>and know that with him died his plans.
>To pull a trigger, heartache make,
>each time I'm forced a life to take.
>To pull a trigger, not recall,
>his final cry before his fall.

IV I think of all who fought and died,
those stood against me, those beside.
>I think of them and what they'd be,
>their futures lost for them to see.
>I think of daughters, wives and sons,
>of all the things they've left undone.
>**I think that they too thought of me**
>**and pray a demon did not see.**

The following poem is dedicated to the
memory of CSM W. E. Howe

Free To Roam

I   If this must be the day I die,
don't wail for me, no mournful sigh.

    For freedom finds me free to roam,
above the sundrenched fields of home.

III   And when in time you come to dream,
of long lost things or it may seem.

    Look to the brook, its waves and flow,
the windswept drifts and mounds of snow.

V   For these are things for which I fight,
that evil leaves with bloodied blight.

    For you to walk on pastures green,
to live the life as yet unseen.

VII   And all I ask is don't forget,
and live each day without regret.

    As each day dawns and nighttime falls,
remember those who gave their all.

*"Tell me are you still my own,
with faithful eyes and constant heart."*

The depth of our love is often unknown until the hour of separation. Rarely do we know how strong we will be without our loved ones until we are forced to bring that hidden strength forward. What separation could be greater than the divide of war and how easy it is for a kernel of doubt to take hold.

Stephan I Myers

Old Man Out

Tell me do you think of me,
as often as I do of you.
Your picture clutched to troubled breast,
while nightmares tear my sleep in two.

II

Tell me when I cross your mind,
does separations anguish hurt,
or do you flutter lashes wide
and look for men with which to flirt?

III

Tell me are you still my own,
with faithful eyes and constant heart,
or does your window sill proclaim,
the absence of your counterpart.

IV

Tell me do you serve your tea
to lady friends who come to call,
or are you in some alleyway,
your passion spent against the wall?

V

Tell me are the sheets still cool,
and clean on my side of the bed,
or are they rumpled up with sex
from all the men your love has fed?

VI

Tell me love when I return,
with weary step and shattered mind,
to fall exhausted in your arms.
What kind of woman will I find?

Her Reply

I   Affection starved and insecure.
This mind denying sleeps allure.

       While sinking fast beneath the blue,
with outstretched fingers seeking you.

III   Connection made twixt eyes and heart.
Its anguish causing them to smart.

       Uncertain thoughts return to gloat.
Your letter binding up my throat.

V   Remembered closeness in the past,
both tangible and fading fast.

       The chasm grows with dizzy speed,
of loves entreaty takes no heed.

VII   A hedge of thorns around my soul,
which wars indifference came and stole.

       No touch, no look or lover's tease.
No holding hands with passion's squeeze.

IX   Tis true my heart began to mourn,
warm promises your tongue has sworn.

             Once weighted down by longing's shroud,
I read yours words and laughed out loud.

XI   The parts of me at which you smiled,
unknowingly your heart beguiled.

             Entrenched are they behind closed doors.
My love is yours forevermore.

Poised To Fire

I   Poised to fire, my trigger taut,
your life is in my hands.

II   On sun soaked sands
where once grew wheat,
where sounds the guns
and good men meet.

III   Turn back the clock
and linger there.
Put down your arms
and breathe the air.

IV   How did we fall
so far from grace,
to covet hate
in face and race?

V   Poised to fire, your trigger taut,
my life is in your hands.

"Their children orphaned, wives bereft.
A photograph is all that's left."

We live in a world that has borders and those borders need to be guarded. The very least we can do for our military men and women is to honor and be grateful for the sacrifices they make so we might prosper.

Stephan J Myers

The Hero

I ***That blaze of glory, hero's death.***
The sacrifice of final breath.

The pain within that last release,
to liberate and fight for peace.

And in those moments does he think,
while teetering on fated brink.

His life was worth his country's pride-
this fractured world for which he died.

Flickering image, news to tell,
of foreign shores on which you fell.

VI City streets where life goes by,
where no one thinks to question why.

A morning's news, a two page spread,
is all we give to mourn the dead.

Their children orphaned, wives bereft.
A photograph is all that's left.

With faded hue it sits meanwhile,
amongst her children's laughing smile.

X ***She passes by, her eyes still wet.***
The only one who won't forget.

∞

Men Of War

I

We humans standing tall, upright,
proclaim intelligence and might.

We found the fire, we made the wheel,
the weaponry with which to steal.

We're living proof of God's success;
the crème de crème of nature's best.

We climbed the ladder, scaled the heights.
Came out on top, to our delight.

V

Just look at all the things we've done,
from swim, to crawl, to walk, to run.

We've cars and trains and things that fly,
and buildings towering to the sky.

We've bombs and bullets, swords and knives,
to mutilate and ruin lives.

Our kinship lost with broken trust,
in bloody patriotic lust.

IX

But still our haughty necks we raise.
Destroy our brothers in a blaze.

Congratulate and pat our backs,
while killing kids in air attacks.

Superior to other life,
we love to hate and live in strife.

Whilst on they look with saddened eyes,
their wisdom lost amongst our lies.

*"Around the fallen soldiers neck,
a cross shines bright,
against the dark."*

The dictates of religion teach us that
the true soldier fights not because he
hates what is in front of him, but
because he loves what is behind him.
Can religion and war really be so
easily reconciled?

Stephan J Myers

The Padre

I **The padre stands, his robes hang long,**
pale figure in the candle-light.
>One hand rests soft on downy heads.
>His many rings glint cold and bright.

He lifts his voice to call his God,
with passions strength, his timbre deep.
>Imbues with spirit those before,
>persuading them their faith to keep.

III He promises the hand of God
to hold their own when 'ere they fight,
>and urges them when all is dark,
>to keep belief before them bright.

He sends them off with guns and tanks-
the ten commandments mentioned not.
>Their aim to kill their fellowman.
>The sixth command they all forgot.

V And when the young man lifts his gun,
the bullet seeking out its mark.
>**Around the fallen soldiers neck,**
>**a cross shines bright, against the dark.**

*"Put down your arms
and breathe the air."*

If we must go to war, then let it be against an enemy who would destroy everything we hold dear. But pray we never come to love the sound of battle, the gun for its range, the stealth of the bombs we drop, nor medals for their glory.

Stephan J Myers

This Veil

I have gathered myself from everywhere.
From memories of battles here and there.

To know beyond doubt this man that I am.
And reveal the truth of God's veiled plan.

Beyond the swaggering of war's intent.
Strife without end and feigned repent.

For such have I mustered to cheat despair.
Compassion spent and devoid of care.

V

Distant memories conspired to deceive.
Honour, my want in which I believed.

Now in blunt stillness of that dissension,
I seek, nay demand, comprehension.

To see as I'm seen and know as I'm known.
When last breath's spent and lungs are blown.

So those that have loved me may lift this veil.
This soldier aside, to know me well.

Fallen Foe

O Enemy, my fallen foe,
our war is fought, our gauntlet run.

Our hearts endured, our aim was true.
Our battles lost and won.

As home draws near, their cheers I hear,
our kin now celebrating.

Whilst heavy weighs this leaden heart,
my thoughts not fit for sharing.

V

But foe, my foe. My fallen foe!
Your blood ran truly thick and red.

Where there on distant arid ground,
your corpse fell cold and dead.

O Enemy, my fallen foe,
if you were here not me.

Would you think the price we paid
had really set us free?

IX

Beloved ones amidst the crowd,
their happy faces turning.

Waving banners, hands held high,
our touch for which they're yearning.

But foe, my foe. My fallen foe!
No pumping heart or stealthy tread.

Your lips turned blue, your voice now still.
Your corpse now cold and dead.

The following poem is dedicated to the
memory of Flt Lt VJC Miles DFC and Pilot
Officer Ferdie Perry DFC

Armistice

I

I walk apart, this strange new world,
no brothers by my side.
With shoulders back and head held high,
dark terrors do I hide.

No guns, no bombs, no chilling screams,
no bodies do I see.
I walk these streets that know no fear,
no longer to be me.

III

A wraithlike man who walks alone,
no home to call my own.
A listless nomad forged in war,
where these dark seeds were sown.

Ahead a field of white washed stones,
where few now care to tread.
Where walk the ghosts that fell with me,
the fated fallen dead.

V

No heroes here, just plucky souls,
who rose when times were dire.
For near and dear we gave our all
and fell before the wire.

I see my name, so stark and plain,
a century now has past.
All good intent, just words to me,
pray armistice will last.

*"Why do we fight for
a piece of this earth?"*

No one hates war more than the soldier
who has lived it and intimately knows
its brutality. Every gun that is loaded,
every warship launched, every rocket
fired, heralds the loss of a life. The theft
of a future filled with promise. Yet it's
the very act of war that preserves our
right to ask if it is wrong or right.
Perhaps all we can ever say is that war
should never be advocated except as a
means of peace.

Stephan J Myers

What Did I Die For?

I   What did I die for,
what did I gain?
Saving this world,
so that others could maim.

II   Where are my comrades?
Asleep in the ground.
Their spirits forgotten.
Their souls never found.

III   Why do we fight for
a piece of this earth?
When we treat it so badly
and plunder its worth.

IV   When did we humans
get hungry with greed?
Turning backs on our brothers,
denying their needs.

V   How can the tramping
of time be turned back,
to relive and repair
and make new what we lack?

THE END.

A Message From Stephan

In my "Briefest Of Introductions" I shared my hope that with these words we would touch your heart and mind, that somewhere along this journey we call life our thoughts would briefly bring us together and the sacrifices of so many will never be forgotten.

It's unlikely we will see the end to all wars in our lifetime but by keeping the memory of our fallen alive we ensure the flame of hope never dies.

Till next time,

Stephan.

Discover The Poetry Of Thief Of Hearts

"A poignant collection of verse, to be read slowly, in a quiet place and savoured. And, with a box of tissues!"

"Wow, how many of us can relate to the poems contained in Thief Of Hearts? I would say, all of us. We've all had our hearts broken. Truly heart wrenching."

"A truly beautiful but heart breaking read. Anyone who has ever loved and lost someone dear and essential to them cannot fail to be moved by the words."

"Capturing all of these painful moments as well as capturing what is so fantastic about love. Brilliant!"

"The wait was most certainly worth it.... As soon as I started to read I knew I wasn't going to put it down until I had finished!"

"Myers' words wrap around the mind like a lover's fingers intertwined. Whether you're someone who's loved and lost or still in the throes of that most confusing emotion, "love", then this is the book to try and make sense of it all!"

Thief Of Hearts

Poetry For Those Who Have Loved,
Lost and Dared To Love Again.

Trust In All My Charms

I

Against my breast I'll hold you tight,
encircled in my arms.

As piece by piece I'll mend your heart
and keep you safe from harm.

Be sure I'll never leave you,
these bonds are strong and sure.

For all my life I'll love you true,
my ward for evermore.

V

On blackest days when spirits fall,
to plumb depths of despair.

No need to turn or call my name
for I am always there.

Whitest knight in armour bright,
your paladin made real.

When head is hanging leaden,
for my love is forged in steel.

IX

When wraiths and words beset you
and heavy weighs your crown.

I'll lift you up and hold you high,
your fool and loving clown.

And in return, not much I'll ask,
just hold me in your arms.

To steer the truest course you can
and trust in all my charms.

The Nightmares Fade

I

No separation here exists
between your soul and mine.

Each nourished by the other's breath
as spirits both combine.

III

Without your presence light grows dim
as gloom consumes my mind.

It hibernates in deathly cold,
leaves happiness behind.

V

But with you near my flesh grows warm,
my mind is free to roam.

As in your arms the nightmares fade.
For you, my dear, are home.

A Ghostly Kiss

I

The hollow nestled at your throat
for me to gently kiss.
Your lips against my forehead rest
and I am lost to bliss.

II

So lightly do my lips caress,
as fires rage within.
These kisses sultry and divine,
my palm beneath your chin.

III

A simple thing for us to do
and yet within each kiss,
resides the sum of all we are
and all our hearts would miss.

IV

Your face now tilted, eyes are closed,
your neck you come to bare.
Lost in moments gone to quick,
you vanish into air.

∞

Also By Stephan J Myers

Thief Of Hearts

Loss De Plott & The Colour Red

Loss De Plot & The Colour Blue

Loss De Plott & The Colour Gold

Loss De Plott & A Bear Called Ted

Loss De Plott & The Golden Scroll

The Clockwork Emporium

The Colour Red Plotter's Edition

Website

www.StephanJMyers.com

Getting in touch by email.

contact@StephanJMyers.com

Printed in Great Britain
by Amazon

39235952R00086